Magnificent Monarchs

Magnificent Monarchs

by Linda Glaser

illustrated by Gay Holland

THE MILLBROOK PRESS

BROOKFIELD, CONNECTICUT

Look what I found here in these weeds.
A shiny white egg stuck on a leaf.

A tiny monarch caterpillar pushes her way out,
my soft and wiggly friend.

She eats and eats the milkweed leaves.
She grows and grows until…

she grows right out of her small tight skin.
She now has a bigger, looser one.

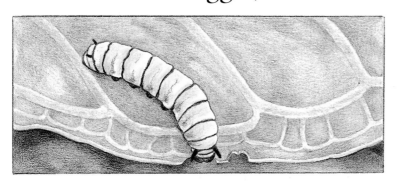

She eats more and more milkweed and then...

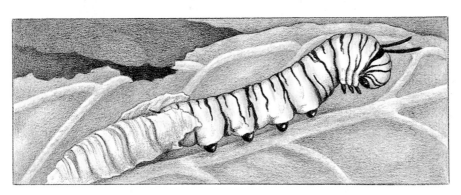

she grows right out of her skin again...

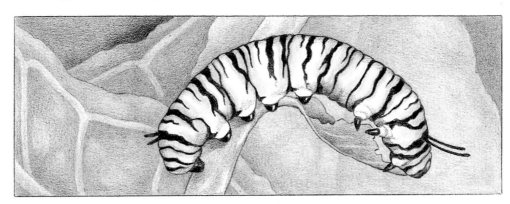

and again...

and AGAIN.

Now she finds a safe place
in the shade and hangs
upside down like a "J."

She sheds her skin once more. And look!
A chrysalis has formed.

My little friend is safe inside.
She stays in there for days and days,
while her whole body changes
in wonderful ways.

When she comes out she's not fat or wiggly. She's become a monarch butterfly with magnificent wings. Now she's ready for an amazing journey.

It's autumn. She must not get cold.
She quickly heads south for a warm
winter home.

She flies day after day and
sips nectar from flowering weeds
on the way.

She meets other monarchs all heading south. They gather like tan and orange leaves, resting a while on "butterfly trees."

On and on my little friend goes,
flying thousands of miles to Mexico.
What an amazing flight
for a little one so thin and light!

Millions of monarchs gather here, where all their great-grandparents came last year.

They all rest, close together, staying warm until spring. Then my little friend starts back north again.

Here she finds young
milkweed plants. She lays
her eggs. At last!

Soon a wiggly caterpillar
pushes out of the egg,
a tiny new life, an
amazing new friend.

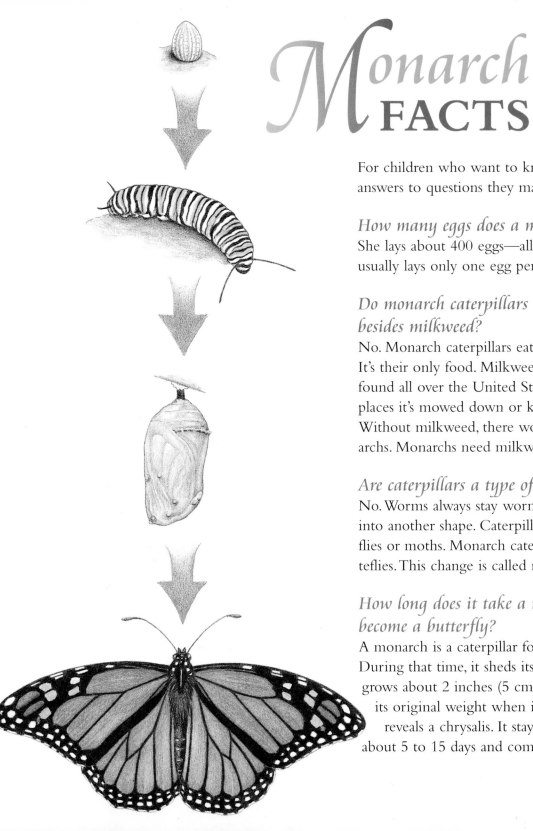

Monarch FACTS

For children who want to know more, here are some answers to questions they may have:

How many eggs does a monarch butterfly lay?
She lays about 400 eggs—all on milkweed plants. She usually lays only one egg per plant.

Do monarch caterpillars eat any other plants besides milkweed?
No. Monarch caterpillars eat only milkweed leaves. It's their only food. Milkweed is a common weed found all over the United States. However, in many places it's mowed down or killed because it's a weed. Without milkweed, there would be no more monarchs. Monarchs need milkweed to survive.

Are caterpillars a type of worm?
No. Worms always stay worms. They never change into another shape. Caterpillars change into butterflies or moths. Monarch caterpillars change into butteflies. This change is called metamorphosis.

How long does it take a monarch caterpillar to become a butterfly?
A monarch is a caterpillar for about two weeks. During that time, it sheds its skin four times and grows about 2 inches (5 cm) long. It is 3,000 times its original weight when it sheds once more and reveals a chrysalis. It stays inside the chrysalis about 5 to 15 days and comes out a butterfly.

What are "butterfly trees"?

The trees where the monarch butterflies gather on their way south during migration are called "butterfly trees." Year after year, a totally new generation of monarch butterflies gather in the same grove of trees that their great grandparents gathered in the year before.

Do all monarchs migrate?

No. Only monarchs born in autumn in North America migrate. They live much longer than other monarchs—about eight months—and fly thousands of miles south to winter in either California or Mexico. In California, monarchs overwinter in many sites along the coast, including San Luis Obispo, Santa Cruz, and Pacific Grove. In Mexico, millions of monarchs gather in huge masses that cover the treees and ground in the oyamel forests in the Sierra Madre mountains. They stay there all winter to keep warm. In spring, they fly back north to lay their eggs. This is the end of their long and remarkable life.

Do migrating monarchs fly all the way back where they were born?

Probably not. A few strong ones may. But most fly partway north, lay eggs, and die. The next generation flies farther north, lays eggs, and dies and so on—like a relay race. There are about three generations of summer monarchs. They each live about a month or so. Then the autumn generation is born. They are the new migrating monarchs. Those born east of the Rocky Mountains or in southern Canada migrate to Mexico. Those born west of the Rockies migrate to California.

How do migrating monarchs find their way?

This is a mystery. Each year, migrating monarchs fly thousands of miles. For all of them it's their first and only trip. Yet they find their way to the same overwintering sites that their great-grandparents found the year before! Some scientists think they do it by sensing the magnetic pull of the Earth or by solar navigation. But no one really knows.

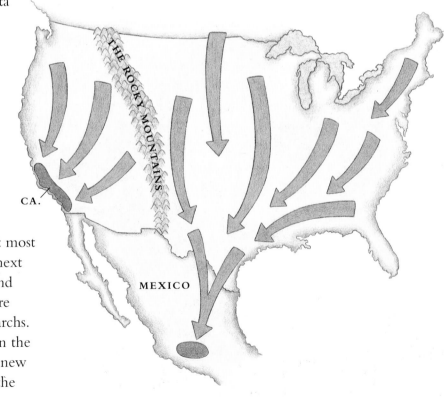

How do monarchs fly so far with such thin wings and thin bodies?

They stop and sip nectar for energy. When they can, they let warm air currents (thermals) and winds carry them. Still, it's an amazing journey for such small, light, fragile-looking creatures.

What do monarch butterflies eat?

Monarch butterflies sip nectar (the sweet juice) of plants such as dandelions, milkweed, thistle, phlox, and wild aster. Their mouth— a proboscis—is shaped like a long skinny straw. It curls up when they're not eating and uncurls to sip the nectar.

What makes monarchs so special?

The monarch is the only tropical butterfly that lives part of its life far from the tropics—in places all over the United States and southern Canada. The monarch of North America is the only known butterfly that migrates to specific destinations in large numbers and makes a two-way journey. Migrating monarchs are threatened.

Are there other monarchs besides migrating monarchs?

Yes. Some monarchs live their entire lives in tropical locations such as Florida, southern Mexico, and Central America.

Are all monarchs threatened?

Monarchs that live their whole lives in the tropics are not threatened but migrating monarchs that live part of their lives in North America are threatened because of:

- Bug sprays and weed killers (herbicides, pesticides, insecticides)—These poisons sprayed on fields and in people's yards kill monarch caterpillars and butterflies.

- Loss of habitats—Many monarch over-wintering sites have been cleared for development in California, and for logging and agriculture in Mexico. Many others are in danger of being destroyed. To survive, migrating monarchs need the remaining sites in California and Mexico protected.

How can we help protect our migrating monarchs?

- Learn about monarchs and share what you know with others.

- Plant a "butterfly flower garden" with big clumps of yellow, orange, red, and purple flowers to attract monarchs. Garden organically (without using weed or bug sprays.)

- Buy organic food that was grown without using bug or weed killers

- Support organizations working to protect migrating monarchs:

  The Monarch Butterfly Sanctuary
      Foundation
  2078 Shillman Ave.
  Roseville, MN 55113
  www.mbsf.org

Where can I find out more about monarchs?

For "hands on" learning write to:

Monarchs in the Classroom
Department of Ecology, Evolution, and Behavior
University of Minnesota
1987 Upper Burford Circle
St. Paul, MN 55108
www.monarchlab.umn.edu

To follow the actual monarch migration, visit Journey North Web site:
www.learner.org/jnorth

To learn more, visit Monarch Watch Web site: www.Monarchwatch.org

West Coast monarch watchers can visit The Friends of Monarchs at
www.pgmonarchs.org/foms.html.

For more information write to:
The Xerces Society
4828 Southeast Hawthorne Blvd.
Portland, OR 97215

To teachers everywhere who bring the wonder
and magic of monarchs into their classrooms.

—L.G.

In memory of my father, H. Bowen Willman,
geologist extraordinaire, who gave me his love
of the natural world.

—G.W.H.

Library of Congress Cataloging-in-Publication Data
Glaser, Linda.
Magnificent monarchs / by Linda Glaser.
p. cm.
Summary: Describes, in simple text and illustrations, the
physical characteristics, habits, and life cycle of the monarch
butterfly.
ISBN 0-7613-1700-7 (lib. bdg.) 0-7613-1636-1 (pbk.)
1. Monarch butterfly—Juvenile literature. [1. Monarch but-
terfly. 2. Butterflies.]
I. Title.
QL561.D3 G63 2000 595.78'9—dc21 99-086640

Published by The Millbrook Press, Inc.
2 Old New Milford Road
Brookfield, Connecticut 06804
www.millbrookpress.com